50 Low-Carb Dessert Recipes

By: Kelly Johnson

Table of Contents

- Almond Flour Chocolate Cake
- Keto Cheesecake Bites
- Sugar-Free Chocolate Mousse
- Coconut Flour Brownies
- Raspberry Chia Pudding
- Almond Joy Fat Bombs
- Keto Lemon Bars
- No-Bake Peanut Butter Cookies
- Chocolate Avocado Pudding
- Low-Carb Pumpkin Pie
- Keto Cinnamon Rolls
- Coconut Macaroons
- Sugar-Free Panna Cotta
- Keto Chocolate Chip Cookies
- Almond Flour Pancakes
- Berry Almond Crumble
- Sugar-Free Coconut Cream Pie
- Keto Chocolate Lava Cake
- Low-Carb Strawberry Sorbet
- Avocado Chocolate Truffles
- Keto Lemon Cheesecake
- Chocolate Dipped Strawberries
- Chia Seed Vanilla Pudding
- Low-Carb Tiramisu
- No-Bake Keto Cheesecake
- Keto Raspberry Coconut Bars
- Almond Flour Cupcakes
- Sugar-Free Peanut Butter Cups
- Keto Chocolate Bark
- Lemon Coconut Fat Bombs
- Low-Carb Snickerdoodle Cookies
- Keto Pumpkin Muffins
- Sugar-Free Ice Cream
- Chocolate Coconut Truffles
- Keto Strawberry Shortcake

- Low-Carb Mocha Cheesecake
- Cinnamon Roll Fat Bombs
- Keto Pecan Pie
- Sugar-Free Lemonade Popsicles
- Low-Carb Almond Joy Bars
- Keto Chocolate Peanut Butter Fudge
- Sugar-Free Cheesecake Bars
- Coconut Almond Fat Bombs
- Keto Churros
- No-Bake Chocolate Peanut Butter Balls
- Low-Carb Mocha Cake
- Keto Coconut Milk Fudge
- Sugar-Free Chocolate Chip Blondies
- Chocolate Raspberry Cheesecake
- Keto Almond Cake

Almond Flour Chocolate Cake

Ingredients:

- 1 1/2 cups almond flour
- 1/2 cup unsweetened cocoa powder
- 1 tsp baking powder
- 1/2 tsp baking soda
- 1/4 tsp salt
- 4 large eggs
- 1/2 cup unsweetened almond milk
- 1/2 cup erythritol or preferred sweetener
- 1/2 tsp vanilla extract
- 1/4 cup melted coconut oil
- 1/4 cup sugar-free chocolate chips (optional)

Instructions:

1. Preheat the oven to 350°F (175°C). Grease an 8-inch round cake pan or line it with parchment paper.
2. In a large bowl, whisk together almond flour, cocoa powder, baking powder, baking soda, and salt.
3. In another bowl, whisk the eggs, almond milk, erythritol, vanilla extract, and melted coconut oil.
4. Combine the wet and dry ingredients, mixing until smooth. Fold in chocolate chips if desired.
5. Pour the batter into the prepared pan and bake for 20-25 minutes or until a toothpick inserted into the center comes out clean.
6. Allow the cake to cool completely before serving.

Keto Cheesecake Bites

Ingredients:

- 8 oz cream cheese, softened
- 1/4 cup sour cream
- 1/4 cup powdered erythritol
- 1 tsp vanilla extract
- 1/4 cup unsweetened almond butter
- 1/4 cup crushed almonds or your favorite nuts (optional)

Instructions:

1. In a mixing bowl, combine the softened cream cheese, sour cream, powdered erythritol, vanilla extract, and almond butter. Beat until smooth and creamy.
2. Scoop the mixture into small bite-sized balls using a spoon or cookie scoop.
3. Roll the cheesecake bites in crushed almonds or other nuts if desired.
4. Place them on a baking sheet lined with parchment paper and refrigerate for at least 2 hours before serving.

Sugar-Free Chocolate Mousse

Ingredients:

- 1/2 cup heavy whipping cream
- 1/4 cup unsweetened cocoa powder
- 2 tbsp powdered erythritol (or your preferred sweetener)
- 1/2 tsp vanilla extract
- Pinch of salt

Instructions:

1. In a mixing bowl, whisk the heavy whipping cream, cocoa powder, erythritol, vanilla extract, and salt until soft peaks form.
2. Continue whisking until the mousse becomes thick and fluffy.
3. Spoon the mousse into serving dishes and refrigerate for at least 1 hour.
4. Serve chilled, optionally garnished with whipped cream or berries.

Coconut Flour Brownies

Ingredients:

- 1/2 cup coconut flour
- 1/4 cup unsweetened cocoa powder
- 1/2 tsp baking powder
- 1/4 tsp salt
- 3 large eggs
- 1/4 cup melted butter or coconut oil
- 1/4 cup erythritol or preferred sweetener
- 1 tsp vanilla extract
- 1/4 cup unsweetened almond milk
- 1/2 cup sugar-free chocolate chips (optional)

Instructions:

1. Preheat the oven to 350°F (175°C). Grease an 8x8-inch baking pan.
2. In a large bowl, whisk together coconut flour, cocoa powder, baking powder, and salt.
3. In another bowl, whisk the eggs, melted butter or coconut oil, erythritol, vanilla extract, and almond milk.
4. Combine the wet and dry ingredients and mix until smooth. Fold in chocolate chips if desired.
5. Pour the batter into the prepared pan and bake for 20-25 minutes or until a toothpick comes out clean.
6. Allow the brownies to cool before cutting into squares.

Raspberry Chia Pudding

Ingredients:

- 1/2 cup unsweetened almond milk
- 1/4 cup chia seeds
- 1/2 cup fresh raspberries (or more for topping)
- 1 tbsp erythritol or preferred sweetener
- 1/2 tsp vanilla extract

Instructions:

1. In a mixing bowl, combine almond milk, chia seeds, sweetener, and vanilla extract. Stir well to combine.
2. Cover and refrigerate for at least 4 hours or overnight to allow the chia seeds to absorb the liquid and form a pudding-like texture.
3. Serve topped with fresh raspberries or other berries of your choice.

Almond Joy Fat Bombs

Ingredients:

- 1/2 cup unsweetened shredded coconut
- 1/4 cup almond butter
- 2 tbsp coconut oil, melted
- 2 tbsp erythritol or preferred sweetener
- 1/4 cup almonds, whole or chopped
- 2 oz sugar-free dark chocolate

Instructions:

1. In a bowl, mix together shredded coconut, almond butter, melted coconut oil, and erythritol until well combined.
2. Roll the mixture into small balls (about 1-inch size) and press an almond into the center of each.
3. Melt the sugar-free dark chocolate in the microwave or on the stove, then drizzle over the fat bombs.
4. Refrigerate for at least 1 hour before serving.

Keto Lemon Bars

Ingredients:

- For the crust:
    - 1 1/2 cups almond flour
    - 1/4 cup melted butter
    - 2 tbsp erythritol or preferred sweetener
    - 1/4 tsp salt
- For the lemon filling:
    - 3 large eggs
    - 1/2 cup fresh lemon juice
    - 1/4 cup erythritol
    - 2 tbsp coconut flour
    - Zest of 1 lemon

Instructions:

1. Preheat the oven to 350°F (175°C). Grease an 8x8-inch pan.
2. To make the crust, combine almond flour, melted butter, erythritol, and salt. Press the mixture into the bottom of the pan to form a crust.
3. Bake for 10-12 minutes until golden. Remove from the oven.
4. To make the filling, whisk together the eggs, lemon juice, erythritol, coconut flour, and lemon zest.
5. Pour the lemon filling over the crust and bake for 18-20 minutes, until set.
6. Let the bars cool completely before slicing into squares.

No-Bake Peanut Butter Cookies

Ingredients:

- 1/2 cup peanut butter (unsweetened)
- 1/4 cup coconut flour
- 1/4 cup erythritol or preferred sweetener
- 1 tsp vanilla extract
- Pinch of salt
- 1/4 cup unsweetened almond milk

Instructions:

1. In a bowl, combine the peanut butter, coconut flour, erythritol, vanilla extract, salt, and almond milk. Mix until smooth.
2. Roll the mixture into small balls and place them on a parchment-lined baking sheet.
3. Flatten each ball with a fork to create a cookie shape.
4. Refrigerate for at least 1 hour before serving.

Chocolate Avocado Pudding

Ingredients:

- 2 ripe avocados
- 1/4 cup unsweetened cocoa powder
- 1/4 cup erythritol or preferred sweetener
- 1/2 tsp vanilla extract
- 1/4 cup unsweetened almond milk
- Pinch of salt

Instructions:

1. In a blender or food processor, combine the avocados, cocoa powder, erythritol, vanilla extract, almond milk, and salt.
2. Blend until smooth and creamy.
3. Refrigerate for 1 hour before serving. Optionally, garnish with fresh berries or whipped cream.

Low-Carb Pumpkin Pie

Ingredients:

- For the crust:
    - 1 1/2 cups almond flour
    - 1/4 cup coconut flour
    - 1/4 cup butter, melted
    - 1 tbsp erythritol or preferred sweetener
    - 1/4 tsp salt
- For the filling:
    - 2 cups canned pumpkin puree
    - 3 large eggs
    - 1/2 cup unsweetened almond milk
    - 1/2 cup erythritol
    - 1 tsp cinnamon
    - 1/2 tsp ginger
    - 1/4 tsp nutmeg
    - 1/4 tsp cloves
    - 1/4 tsp salt

Instructions:

1. Preheat the oven to 350°F (175°C). Grease a 9-inch pie pan.
2. To make the crust, combine almond flour, coconut flour, melted butter, erythritol, and salt. Press the mixture into the pie pan to form the crust. Bake for 10-12 minutes until golden, then remove from the oven.
3. For the filling, whisk together the pumpkin puree, eggs, almond milk, erythritol, cinnamon, ginger, nutmeg, cloves, and salt.
4. Pour the filling into the pre-baked crust and smooth the top.
5. Bake for 40-45 minutes, or until a toothpick inserted into the center comes out clean.
6. Allow the pie to cool completely before serving.

Keto Cinnamon Rolls

Ingredients:

- For the dough:
    - 2 cups almond flour
    - 1/2 cup coconut flour
    - 2 tsp baking powder
    - 1/4 tsp salt
    - 1/4 cup erythritol
    - 2 large eggs
    - 1/4 cup melted butter
    - 1/4 cup unsweetened almond milk
    - 1 tsp vanilla extract
- For the filling:
    - 1/4 cup softened butter
    - 1/4 cup erythritol
    - 1 tbsp ground cinnamon
- For the glaze:
    - 2 oz cream cheese, softened
    - 2 tbsp butter, softened
    - 1/4 cup powdered erythritol
    - 1 tsp vanilla extract

Instructions:

1. Preheat the oven to 350°F (175°C). Line a baking dish with parchment paper.
2. To make the dough, combine almond flour, coconut flour, baking powder, salt, and erythritol in a large bowl.
3. Add eggs, melted butter, almond milk, and vanilla extract. Mix until a dough forms.
4. Roll the dough out between two sheets of parchment paper into a rectangle shape.
5. Spread softened butter over the dough, then sprinkle with erythritol and cinnamon.
6. Roll the dough tightly and slice into 8 pieces. Place the rolls in the prepared baking dish.
7. Bake for 20-25 minutes until golden and cooked through.
8. To make the glaze, combine cream cheese, butter, erythritol, and vanilla extract. Mix until smooth and drizzle over the warm cinnamon rolls.

Coconut Macaroons

Ingredients:

- 3 cups unsweetened shredded coconut
- 3 large egg whites
- 1/4 cup erythritol or preferred sweetener
- 1 tsp vanilla extract
- Pinch of salt

Instructions:

1. Preheat the oven to 325°F (160°C). Line a baking sheet with parchment paper.
2. In a large bowl, whisk the egg whites until stiff peaks form.
3. Gently fold in the shredded coconut, erythritol, vanilla extract, and salt.
4. Using a spoon, drop spoonfuls of the mixture onto the prepared baking sheet.
5. Bake for 15-18 minutes until the macaroons are golden brown.
6. Allow the macaroons to cool completely before serving.

Sugar-Free Panna Cotta

Ingredients:

- 2 cups heavy whipping cream
- 1/2 cup unsweetened almond milk
- 1/4 cup erythritol or preferred sweetener
- 1 tsp vanilla extract
- 1 tbsp unflavored gelatin
- 2 tbsp cold water

Instructions:

1. In a small bowl, sprinkle the gelatin over cold water and let it bloom for 5 minutes.
2. In a saucepan, combine the heavy whipping cream, almond milk, erythritol, and vanilla extract. Heat over medium heat, stirring until the sweetener dissolves.
3. Remove the mixture from the heat and stir in the bloomed gelatin until completely dissolved.
4. Pour the mixture into serving glasses or ramekins and refrigerate for at least 4 hours, or until set.
5. Serve chilled, optionally with a berry topping or sugar-free fruit compote.

Keto Chocolate Chip Cookies

Ingredients:

- 2 cups almond flour
- 1/2 tsp baking soda
- 1/4 tsp salt
- 1/2 cup butter, softened
- 1/4 cup erythritol or preferred sweetener
- 1 large egg
- 1 tsp vanilla extract
- 1/2 cup sugar-free chocolate chips

Instructions:

1. Preheat the oven to 350°F (175°C). Line a baking sheet with parchment paper.
2. In a bowl, combine almond flour, baking soda, and salt.
3. In a separate bowl, beat together the butter, erythritol, egg, and vanilla extract until smooth.
4. Add the dry ingredients to the wet ingredients and stir until well combined.
5. Fold in the chocolate chips.
6. Drop spoonfuls of the dough onto the prepared baking sheet and flatten slightly.
7. Bake for 10-12 minutes until golden around the edges. Cool before serving.

Almond Flour Pancakes

Ingredients:

- 1 1/2 cups almond flour
- 2 large eggs
- 1/4 cup unsweetened almond milk
- 1 tbsp melted butter
- 1 tsp vanilla extract
- 1/2 tsp baking powder
- Pinch of salt
- Butter or coconut oil for cooking

Instructions:

1. In a bowl, whisk together the almond flour, eggs, almond milk, melted butter, vanilla extract, baking powder, and salt.
2. Heat a non-stick skillet or griddle over medium heat and add butter or coconut oil.
3. Pour about 1/4 cup of batter onto the skillet for each pancake. Cook for 2-3 minutes on each side, until golden and cooked through.
4. Serve with sugar-free syrup or fresh berries.

Berry Almond Crumble

Ingredients:

- For the filling:
    - 2 cups mixed berries (strawberries, blueberries, raspberries)
    - 2 tbsp erythritol or preferred sweetener
    - 1 tbsp lemon juice
- For the topping:
    - 1 1/2 cups almond flour
    - 1/4 cup butter, cold and cut into cubes
    - 1/4 cup erythritol
    - 1/4 tsp cinnamon
    - Pinch of salt

Instructions:

1. Preheat the oven to 350°F (175°C). Grease a baking dish.
2. For the filling, combine the mixed berries, erythritol, and lemon juice in a bowl. Pour into the prepared dish.
3. For the topping, combine almond flour, butter, erythritol, cinnamon, and salt. Use a fork or pastry cutter to blend until the mixture resembles coarse crumbs.
4. Sprinkle the topping over the berries.
5. Bake for 25-30 minutes until the topping is golden brown and the filling is bubbling.
6. Allow to cool slightly before serving.

Sugar-Free Coconut Cream Pie

Ingredients:

- For the crust:
    - 1 1/2 cups almond flour
    - 1/4 cup melted butter
    - 2 tbsp erythritol or preferred sweetener
    - 1/4 tsp salt
- For the filling:
    - 1 1/2 cups unsweetened coconut milk
    - 3/4 cup heavy cream
    - 1/4 cup erythritol
    - 4 large egg yolks
    - 1 tsp vanilla extract
    - 1/2 cup unsweetened shredded coconut

Instructions:

1. Preheat the oven to 350°F (175°C). Grease a pie dish.
2. To make the crust, combine almond flour, melted butter, erythritol, and salt. Press into the pie dish and bake for 10-12 minutes until golden.
3. For the filling, whisk together coconut milk, heavy cream, erythritol, and egg yolks in a saucepan. Heat over medium heat until thickened.
4. Remove from heat and stir in vanilla extract and shredded coconut.
5. Pour the filling into the pre-baked crust and refrigerate for 4 hours.
6. Serve chilled, optionally topped with whipped cream.

Keto Chocolate Lava Cake

Ingredients:

- 1/4 cup unsweetened almond flour
- 1/4 cup unsweetened cocoa powder
- 1/4 cup butter, melted
- 1/4 cup erythritol
- 2 large eggs
- 1 tsp vanilla extract
- 2 oz sugar-free chocolate (for the center)
- Pinch of salt

Instructions:

1. Preheat the oven to 375°F (190°C). Grease 4 ramekins.
2. In a bowl, combine almond flour, cocoa powder, melted butter, erythritol, eggs, vanilla extract, and salt. Mix until smooth.
3. Spoon a little batter into each ramekin. Place a small piece of sugar-free chocolate in the center and cover with the remaining batter.
4. Bake for 12-15 minutes, until the outside is set but the center is still soft.
5. Let cool for 5 minutes before serving.

Low-Carb Strawberry Sorbet

Ingredients:

- 2 cups fresh strawberries, hulled and sliced
- 1/4 cup erythritol or preferred sweetener
- 1/2 cup water
- 1 tsp lemon juice
- 1/2 tsp vanilla extract

Instructions:

1. In a blender or food processor, blend the strawberries, erythritol, water, lemon juice, and vanilla extract until smooth.
2. Pour the mixture into a shallow dish and place it in the freezer.
3. Every 30 minutes, scrape the mixture with a fork to create a slushy texture.
4. Continue until the sorbet is frozen and fluffy.
5. Serve immediately or store in an airtight container in the freezer.

Avocado Chocolate Truffles

Ingredients:

- 1 ripe avocado
- 1/4 cup unsweetened cocoa powder
- 1/4 cup erythritol or preferred sweetener
- 1/2 tsp vanilla extract
- Pinch of salt
- 1/4 cup dark chocolate chips (optional, for coating)

Instructions:

1. In a blender or food processor, blend the avocado until smooth.
2. Add cocoa powder, erythritol, vanilla extract, and salt. Blend until combined.
3. Scoop out small portions and roll them into balls.
4. If desired, melt dark chocolate chips and dip each truffle in the chocolate.
5. Place the truffles on a baking sheet lined with parchment paper and refrigerate for 1-2 hours to firm up.

Keto Lemon Cheesecake

Ingredients:

- For the crust:
    - 1 1/2 cups almond flour
    - 1/4 cup melted butter
    - 2 tbsp erythritol
    - 1/4 tsp salt
- For the filling:
    - 3 8 oz cream cheese, softened
    - 1/2 cup erythritol
    - 3 large eggs
    - 1/2 cup sour cream
    - 1/4 cup fresh lemon juice
    - Zest of 1 lemon
    - 1 tsp vanilla extract

Instructions:

1. Preheat the oven to 325°F (165°C). Grease a 9-inch springform pan.
2. To make the crust, combine almond flour, melted butter, erythritol, and salt. Press the mixture into the bottom of the prepared pan.
3. Bake the crust for 10-12 minutes, then remove from the oven.
4. For the filling, beat the cream cheese and erythritol together until smooth. Add the eggs, sour cream, lemon juice, lemon zest, and vanilla extract. Beat until combined.
5. Pour the filling over the baked crust and smooth the top.
6. Bake for 50-60 minutes until set. Let the cheesecake cool to room temperature, then refrigerate for at least 4 hours before serving.

Chocolate Dipped Strawberries

Ingredients:

- 10-12 fresh strawberries, hulled
- 1/2 cup sugar-free dark chocolate chips
- 1 tbsp coconut oil (optional, for smoothness)

Instructions:

1. Line a baking sheet with parchment paper.
2. In a heatproof bowl, melt the chocolate chips and coconut oil (if using) over a double boiler or in the microwave, stirring frequently.
3. Dip each strawberry into the melted chocolate, coating it evenly.
4. Place the dipped strawberries on the prepared baking sheet.
5. Refrigerate for 30-60 minutes until the chocolate hardens.

Chia Seed Vanilla Pudding

Ingredients:

- 1/4 cup chia seeds
- 1 cup unsweetened almond milk
- 1 tsp vanilla extract
- 1-2 tbsp erythritol or preferred sweetener
- Pinch of salt

Instructions:

1. In a bowl, whisk together the chia seeds, almond milk, vanilla extract, erythritol, and salt.
2. Cover and refrigerate for at least 4 hours or overnight.
3. Stir the pudding before serving to ensure even consistency. Top with berries if desired.

Low-Carb Tiramisu

Ingredients:

- For the mascarpone filling:
    - 1 1/2 cups mascarpone cheese
    - 1 cup heavy cream
    - 1/4 cup erythritol
    - 1 tsp vanilla extract
    - 2 large egg yolks
- For the coffee soak:
    - 1 cup brewed coffee, cooled
    - 1 tbsp rum or coffee liqueur (optional)
- For the ladyfinger alternative:
    - 1 1/2 cups almond flour
    - 2 large eggs
    - 1/4 cup erythritol
    - 1/2 tsp baking powder
    - 1 tsp vanilla extract

Instructions:

1. Preheat the oven to 350°F (175°C). Line a baking sheet with parchment paper.
2. To make the ladyfinger alternative, beat together the eggs and erythritol until frothy. Add almond flour, baking powder, and vanilla extract. Mix until a dough forms.
3. Pipe the dough into long strips and bake for 10-12 minutes until lightly golden.
4. For the filling, whip the mascarpone cheese, heavy cream, erythritol, vanilla extract, and egg yolks until smooth and fluffy.
5. To assemble, dip the almond flour ladyfingers into the coffee soak and layer them in a dish.
6. Spread a layer of mascarpone filling over the ladyfingers. Repeat with another layer.
7. Refrigerate for 4 hours or overnight before serving.

No-Bake Keto Cheesecake

Ingredients:

- For the crust:
    - 1 1/2 cups almond flour
    - 1/4 cup melted butter
    - 2 tbsp erythritol
    - 1/4 tsp salt
- For the filling:
    - 16 oz cream cheese, softened
    - 1 cup heavy cream
    - 1/4 cup erythritol
    - 1 tsp vanilla extract

Instructions:

1. Grease a springform pan and set aside.
2. To make the crust, combine almond flour, melted butter, erythritol, and salt. Press into the bottom of the pan.
3. In a mixing bowl, beat together the cream cheese, heavy cream, erythritol, and vanilla extract until smooth and fluffy.
4. Spread the filling over the crust and smooth the top.
5. Refrigerate for at least 4 hours, or until set.

Keto Raspberry Coconut Bars

Ingredients:

- 1 1/2 cups unsweetened shredded coconut
- 1/4 cup almond flour
- 1/4 cup erythritol
- 1/4 cup coconut oil, melted
- 1/4 cup unsweetened raspberry puree
- 1 tsp vanilla extract

Instructions:

1. Preheat the oven to 350°F (175°C). Line a baking dish with parchment paper.
2. In a bowl, combine shredded coconut, almond flour, erythritol, and melted coconut oil.
3. Press the mixture into the prepared dish.
4. Bake for 10-12 minutes until golden brown.
5. Remove from the oven and spread the raspberry puree over the top. Refrigerate for 1-2 hours before serving.

Almond Flour Cupcakes

Ingredients:

- 2 cups almond flour
- 1/2 cup erythritol
- 1 tsp baking powder
- 1/4 tsp salt
- 3 large eggs
- 1/4 cup unsweetened almond milk
- 1/4 cup melted butter
- 1 tsp vanilla extract

Instructions:

1. Preheat the oven to 350°F (175°C). Line a cupcake pan with paper liners.
2. In a bowl, combine almond flour, erythritol, baking powder, and salt.
3. In another bowl, whisk together the eggs, almond milk, melted butter, and vanilla extract.
4. Pour the wet ingredients into the dry ingredients and mix until smooth.
5. Divide the batter evenly between the cupcake liners.
6. Bake for 18-20 minutes, or until a toothpick inserted into the center comes out clean.
7. Allow to cool before serving.

Sugar-Free Peanut Butter Cups

Ingredients:

- 1/2 cup unsweetened peanut butter
- 1/4 cup coconut oil
- 1/4 cup erythritol (or preferred sweetener)
- 1/2 tsp vanilla extract
- 1/4 cup unsweetened dark chocolate chips (optional for topping)

Instructions:

1. Line a muffin tin with paper liners.
2. In a saucepan over low heat, melt the coconut oil and peanut butter together.
3. Stir in erythritol and vanilla extract until fully combined.
4. Pour the peanut butter mixture evenly into the muffin liners.
5. If desired, melt the dark chocolate chips and drizzle over the peanut butter mixture.
6. Freeze for at least 1-2 hours until firm. Serve chilled.

Keto Chocolate Bark

Ingredients:

- 1 cup unsweetened dark chocolate chips
- 1/4 cup unsweetened almond butter
- 1/4 cup chopped nuts (e.g., almonds, walnuts)
- 2 tbsp unsweetened coconut flakes
- 1 tbsp erythritol (or preferred sweetener)

Instructions:

1. Line a baking sheet with parchment paper.
2. In a microwave-safe bowl, melt the chocolate chips and almond butter together in 20-second intervals, stirring until smooth.
3. Stir in erythritol.
4. Pour the melted chocolate mixture onto the prepared baking sheet and spread it into an even layer.
5. Sprinkle the nuts and coconut flakes on top.
6. Freeze for 1-2 hours or until the bark hardens. Break into pieces and serve.

Lemon Coconut Fat Bombs

Ingredients:

- 1/2 cup unsweetened shredded coconut
- 1/4 cup coconut oil, melted
- 1 tbsp lemon zest
- 2 tbsp lemon juice
- 1 tbsp erythritol (or preferred sweetener)

Instructions:

1. In a bowl, mix the shredded coconut, melted coconut oil, lemon zest, lemon juice, and erythritol.
2. Spoon the mixture into silicone molds or ice cube trays.
3. Freeze for 1-2 hours until firm.
4. Pop the fat bombs out of the molds and store in the freezer.

Low-Carb Snickerdoodle Cookies

Ingredients:

- 1 1/2 cups almond flour
- 1/4 cup erythritol (or preferred sweetener)
- 1/4 tsp baking soda
- 1/4 tsp cinnamon
- Pinch of salt
- 1/4 cup butter, softened
- 1 egg
- 1 tsp vanilla extract
- 2 tbsp cinnamon (for rolling)

Instructions:

1. Preheat the oven to 350°F (175°C). Line a baking sheet with parchment paper.
2. In a bowl, combine the almond flour, erythritol, baking soda, cinnamon, and salt.
3. In another bowl, cream together the butter, egg, and vanilla extract.
4. Mix the wet ingredients with the dry ingredients until a dough forms.
5. Roll the dough into small balls and then roll them in cinnamon.
6. Place on the prepared baking sheet and bake for 10-12 minutes or until golden.
7. Let cool before serving.

Keto Pumpkin Muffins

Ingredients:

- 1 1/2 cups almond flour
- 1/4 cup erythritol (or preferred sweetener)
- 1 tsp baking powder
- 1/2 tsp cinnamon
- 1/4 tsp nutmeg
- 1/4 tsp ginger
- 1/4 tsp salt
- 1/2 cup canned pumpkin
- 2 large eggs
- 1/4 cup unsweetened almond milk
- 1/4 cup melted butter
- 1 tsp vanilla extract

Instructions:

1. Preheat the oven to 350°F (175°C). Line a muffin tin with paper liners.
2. In a bowl, combine almond flour, erythritol, baking powder, cinnamon, nutmeg, ginger, and salt.
3. In another bowl, whisk together the pumpkin, eggs, almond milk, melted butter, and vanilla extract.
4. Mix the wet ingredients with the dry ingredients until well combined.
5. Spoon the batter into the muffin tin, filling each liner about 2/3 full.
6. Bake for 20-25 minutes, or until a toothpick comes out clean.
7. Let cool before serving.

Sugar-Free Ice Cream

Ingredients:

- 2 cups heavy cream
- 1 cup unsweetened almond milk
- 1/4 cup erythritol (or preferred sweetener)
- 1 tsp vanilla extract

Instructions:

1. In a mixing bowl, whisk together heavy cream, almond milk, erythritol, and vanilla extract until the erythritol dissolves.
2. Pour the mixture into an ice cream maker and follow the manufacturer's instructions for churning.
3. Once churned, transfer the ice cream to a container and freeze for 2-3 hours to firm up.
4. Serve chilled.

Chocolate Coconut Truffles

Ingredients:

- 1 cup unsweetened shredded coconut
- 1/4 cup unsweetened cocoa powder
- 1/4 cup coconut oil, melted
- 2 tbsp erythritol (or preferred sweetener)
- 1 tsp vanilla extract

Instructions:

1. In a bowl, mix the shredded coconut, cocoa powder, melted coconut oil, erythritol, and vanilla extract.
2. Roll the mixture into small balls and place on a baking sheet lined with parchment paper.
3. Freeze for 1-2 hours until firm.
4. Serve chilled or at room temperature.

Keto Strawberry Shortcake

Ingredients:

- For the cake:
    - 1 1/2 cups almond flour
    - 1/4 cup erythritol (or preferred sweetener)
    - 1 tsp baking powder
    - 1/4 tsp salt
    - 3 large eggs
    - 1/4 cup unsweetened almond milk
    - 1/4 cup melted butter
    - 1 tsp vanilla extract
- For the topping:
    - 1 cup heavy whipping cream
    - 1 tbsp erythritol (or preferred sweetener)
    - 1 tsp vanilla extract
    - Fresh strawberries, sliced

Instructions:

1. Preheat the oven to 350°F (175°C). Line a baking dish with parchment paper.
2. In a bowl, combine almond flour, erythritol, baking powder, and salt.
3. In another bowl, whisk together eggs, almond milk, melted butter, and vanilla extract.
4. Mix the wet and dry ingredients until combined, then pour into the prepared dish.
5. Bake for 18-20 minutes, or until a toothpick comes out clean.
6. Let the cake cool completely, then slice into individual servings.
7. For the topping, beat the heavy cream with erythritol and vanilla extract until stiff peaks form.
8. Top each serving with whipped cream and fresh strawberries.

Low-Carb Mocha Cheesecake

Ingredients:

- 2 cups almond flour
- 1/4 cup unsweetened cocoa powder
- 1/4 cup erythritol (or preferred sweetener)
- 1/4 cup melted butter
- 3 packages (8 oz each) cream cheese, softened
- 1/4 cup sour cream
- 2 large eggs
- 1/2 cup brewed coffee (cooled)
- 1 tsp vanilla extract
- 1/4 cup erythritol (or preferred sweetener)
- 1/4 cup unsweetened cocoa powder

Instructions:

1. Preheat the oven to 325°F (165°C).
2. In a bowl, combine almond flour, cocoa powder, erythritol, and melted butter. Press into the bottom of a springform pan to create the crust.
3. In a separate bowl, beat the cream cheese, sour cream, eggs, brewed coffee, vanilla extract, erythritol, and cocoa powder until smooth.
4. Pour the filling over the crust and smooth the top.
5. Bake for 50-60 minutes, or until the center is set. Let it cool completely before refrigerating for at least 4 hours.
6. Serve chilled.

Cinnamon Roll Fat Bombs

Ingredients:

- 1 cup almond flour
- 1/4 cup coconut flour
- 1/4 cup unsweetened almond butter
- 1/4 cup unsweetened coconut oil, melted
- 1/4 cup erythritol (or preferred sweetener)
- 1 tsp ground cinnamon
- 1/2 tsp vanilla extract
- Pinch of salt

Instructions:

1. In a bowl, combine almond flour, coconut flour, cinnamon, erythritol, and salt.
2. Add almond butter, melted coconut oil, and vanilla extract. Stir until fully combined.
3. Roll the dough into small balls and place them on a baking sheet lined with parchment paper.
4. Freeze for 1-2 hours until firm.
5. Serve chilled.

Keto Pecan Pie

Ingredients:

- 2 cups pecan halves
- 1/2 cup unsweetened almond flour
- 1/4 cup erythritol (or preferred sweetener)
- 1/4 cup unsweetened butter, melted
- 3 large eggs
- 1 tsp vanilla extract
- 1/4 cup heavy cream
- 1/4 cup sugar-free maple syrup

Instructions:

1. Preheat the oven to 350°F (175°C).
2. In a bowl, combine almond flour, erythritol, and melted butter. Press into the bottom of a pie pan.
3. In a separate bowl, whisk together eggs, vanilla extract, heavy cream, and sugar-free maple syrup.
4. Stir in the pecans and pour the mixture over the crust.
5. Bake for 30-35 minutes or until the filling is set and slightly browned. Let cool completely before serving.

Sugar-Free Lemonade Popsicles

Ingredients:

- 1 cup fresh lemon juice
- 1/4 cup erythritol (or preferred sweetener)
- 1 cup water
- 1/2 tsp lemon zest

Instructions:

1. In a bowl, whisk together lemon juice, erythritol, water, and lemon zest until the erythritol dissolves.
2. Pour the mixture into popsicle molds.
3. Freeze for 4-6 hours or until solid.
4. Unmold and serve chilled.

Low-Carb Almond Joy Bars

Ingredients:

- 1 cup unsweetened shredded coconut
- 1/4 cup unsweetened almond butter
- 1/4 cup coconut oil, melted
- 1/4 cup erythritol (or preferred sweetener)
- 1/4 cup whole almonds
- 1/4 cup unsweetened dark chocolate chips

Instructions:

1. In a bowl, combine shredded coconut, almond butter, melted coconut oil, and erythritol.
2. Press the mixture into a lined baking pan, forming a solid base.
3. Place whole almonds on top of the coconut mixture.
4. In a separate bowl, melt the dark chocolate chips and pour over the almond layer.
5. Freeze for 1-2 hours until firm. Cut into bars and serve chilled.

Keto Chocolate Peanut Butter Fudge

Ingredients:

- 1/2 cup unsweetened peanut butter
- 1/4 cup unsweetened cocoa powder
- 1/4 cup coconut oil, melted
- 1/4 cup erythritol (or preferred sweetener)
- 1 tsp vanilla extract

Instructions:

1. In a bowl, combine peanut butter, cocoa powder, melted coconut oil, erythritol, and vanilla extract.
2. Mix until smooth and well combined.
3. Pour the mixture into a lined baking pan and spread evenly.
4. Freeze for 2-3 hours until firm.
5. Cut into squares and serve chilled.

Sugar-Free Cheesecake Bars

Ingredients:

- 2 cups almond flour
- 1/4 cup unsweetened butter, melted
- 1/4 cup erythritol (or preferred sweetener)
- 2 packages (8 oz each) cream cheese, softened
- 2 large eggs
- 1/4 cup sour cream
- 1 tsp vanilla extract
- 1/4 cup erythritol (or preferred sweetener)

Instructions:

1. Preheat the oven to 350°F (175°C). Line an 8x8 baking dish with parchment paper.
2. In a bowl, combine almond flour, melted butter, and erythritol. Press into the bottom of the prepared dish.
3. In a separate bowl, beat the cream cheese, eggs, sour cream, vanilla extract, and erythritol until smooth.
4. Pour the cheesecake filling over the crust and smooth the top.
5. Bake for 20-25 minutes, or until the center is set.
6. Let cool completely before refrigerating for at least 2 hours. Cut into bars and serve chilled.

Coconut Almond Fat Bombs

Ingredients:

- 1 cup unsweetened shredded coconut
- 1/4 cup unsweetened almond butter
- 1/4 cup coconut oil, melted
- 1/4 cup erythritol (or preferred sweetener)
- 1/4 cup whole almonds

Instructions:

1. In a bowl, combine shredded coconut, almond butter, melted coconut oil, and erythritol.
2. Roll the mixture into small balls and place them on a baking sheet lined with parchment paper.
3. Place an almond in the center of each ball.
4. Freeze for 1-2 hours until firm.
5. Serve chilled.

Keto Churros

Ingredients:

- 1 1/2 cups almond flour
- 1/2 cup coconut flour
- 1 tsp baking powder
- 1/2 tsp cinnamon
- 1/4 cup unsweetened almond milk
- 1/4 cup melted butter
- 1/4 cup erythritol (or preferred sweetener)
- 1/2 tsp vanilla extract
- Cinnamon and erythritol mixture for coating

Instructions:

1. Preheat the oven to 350°F (175°C). Line a baking sheet with parchment paper.
2. In a bowl, combine almond flour, coconut flour, baking powder, and cinnamon.
3. In a separate bowl, mix almond milk, melted butter, erythritol, and vanilla extract.
4. Add the wet ingredients to the dry ingredients and mix until a dough forms.
5. Transfer the dough to a piping bag with a star tip and pipe churro shapes onto the baking sheet.
6. Bake for 15-20 minutes or until golden brown.
7. Coat the churros in the cinnamon and erythritol mixture before serving.

No-Bake Chocolate Peanut Butter Balls

Ingredients:

- 1 cup unsweetened peanut butter
- 1/2 cup unsweetened shredded coconut
- 1/4 cup almond flour
- 2 tbsp coconut oil, melted
- 1/4 cup erythritol (or preferred sweetener)
- 1/2 cup unsweetened dark chocolate chips

Instructions:

1. In a bowl, combine peanut butter, shredded coconut, almond flour, melted coconut oil, and erythritol. Stir until fully combined.
2. Roll the mixture into small balls and place them on a baking sheet lined with parchment paper.
3. Melt the dark chocolate chips in a microwave or double boiler. Drizzle over the peanut butter balls.
4. Refrigerate for 1-2 hours until firm.
5. Serve chilled.

Low-Carb Mocha Cake

Ingredients:

- 1 1/2 cups almond flour
- 1/4 cup unsweetened cocoa powder
- 1/2 cup erythritol (or preferred sweetener)
- 1 tsp baking powder
- 1/4 tsp salt
- 2 large eggs
- 1/2 cup brewed coffee (cooled)
- 1/4 cup unsweetened almond milk
- 1 tsp vanilla extract
- 1/4 cup melted butter

Instructions:

1. Preheat the oven to 350°F (175°C). Grease an 8-inch round cake pan.
2. In a bowl, combine almond flour, cocoa powder, erythritol, baking powder, and salt.
3. Add the eggs, brewed coffee, almond milk, vanilla extract, and melted butter. Mix until smooth.
4. Pour the batter into the prepared cake pan and smooth the top.
5. Bake for 25-30 minutes, or until a toothpick inserted into the center comes out clean.
6. Let the cake cool before serving.

Keto Coconut Milk Fudge

Ingredients:

- 1/2 cup coconut milk (full-fat)
- 1/4 cup unsweetened shredded coconut
- 1/4 cup erythritol (or preferred sweetener)
- 1/4 cup unsweetened coconut oil, melted
- 1/2 tsp vanilla extract
- Pinch of salt

Instructions:

1. In a saucepan, combine coconut milk, shredded coconut, erythritol, coconut oil, vanilla extract, and salt.
2. Heat over low heat, stirring constantly until the mixture thickens and the erythritol dissolves.
3. Pour the mixture into a lined baking pan and smooth the top.
4. Refrigerate for 2-3 hours until firm.
5. Cut into squares and serve chilled.

Sugar-Free Chocolate Chip Blondies

Ingredients:

- 2 cups almond flour
- 1/2 cup unsweetened almond butter
- 1/4 cup erythritol (or preferred sweetener)
- 2 large eggs
- 1/4 cup unsweetened chocolate chips
- 1 tsp vanilla extract
- 1/4 tsp baking soda
- Pinch of salt

Instructions:

1. Preheat the oven to 350°F (175°C). Line a baking dish with parchment paper.
2. In a bowl, combine almond flour, almond butter, erythritol, eggs, vanilla extract, baking soda, and salt. Stir until smooth.
3. Fold in the chocolate chips.
4. Pour the batter into the prepared baking dish and spread evenly.
5. Bake for 18-20 minutes, or until golden and set.
6. Let cool before cutting into bars.

Chocolate Raspberry Cheesecake

Ingredients:

- 2 cups almond flour
- 1/4 cup unsweetened cocoa powder
- 1/4 cup erythritol (or preferred sweetener)
- 1/4 cup unsweetened butter, melted
- 2 packages (8 oz each) cream cheese, softened
- 1/4 cup sour cream
- 1/4 cup erythritol (or preferred sweetener)
- 1 tsp vanilla extract
- 1/2 cup fresh raspberries

Instructions:

1. Preheat the oven to 325°F (165°C). Line a springform pan with parchment paper.
2. In a bowl, combine almond flour, cocoa powder, erythritol, and melted butter. Press into the bottom of the prepared pan.
3. In a separate bowl, beat the cream cheese, sour cream, erythritol, and vanilla extract until smooth.
4. Pour the cream cheese mixture over the crust and smooth the top.
5. Dot the cheesecake with raspberries and gently swirl with a knife.
6. Bake for 30-35 minutes, or until the center is set. Let cool before refrigerating for 4 hours or overnight.
7. Serve chilled.

Keto Almond Cake

Ingredients:

- 2 cups almond flour
- 1/4 cup erythritol (or preferred sweetener)
- 1/2 tsp baking powder
- 1/4 tsp salt
- 1/2 cup unsweetened almond milk
- 4 large eggs
- 1/4 cup melted butter
- 1 tsp vanilla extract

Instructions:

1. Preheat the oven to 350°F (175°C). Grease a round cake pan.
2. In a bowl, combine almond flour, erythritol, baking powder, and salt.
3. Add almond milk, eggs, melted butter, and vanilla extract. Mix until smooth.
4. Pour the batter into the prepared cake pan and smooth the top.
5. Bake for 25-30 minutes, or until a toothpick inserted into the center comes out clean.
6. Let the cake cool before serving.